His Grace the Duke of Wharton's speech in the House of Lords, on the third reading of the Bill to inflict pains and penalties on Francis (late) Lord Bishop of Rochester; May the 15th, 1723.

Philip Wharton

PRINT EDITIONS

His Grace the Duke of Wharton's speech in the House of Lords, on the third reading of the Bill to inflict pains and penalties on Francis (late) Lord Bishop of Rochester; May the 15th, 1723.

Wharton, Philip Wharton, Duke of
ESTCID: T053619
Reproduction from British Library
The printer's ornament on the titlepage contains a cherub's head with a basket of fruit. Reissued in 1723 with a new titlepage having a printer's ornament containing the bust of a woman, and a full stop following 'May the 15th' in the title.
London : printed for T. Warner, 1723.
25,[1]p. ; 2°

Gale ECCO Print Editions

Relive history with *Eighteenth Century Collections Online*, now available in print for the independent historian and collector. This series includes the most significant English-language and foreign-language works printed in Great Britain during the eighteenth century, and is organized in seven different subject areas including literature and language; medicine, science, and technology; and religion and philosophy. The collection also includes thousands of important works from the Americas.

The eighteenth century has been called "The Age of Enlightenment." It was a period of rapid advance in print culture and publishing, in world exploration, and in the rapid growth of science and technology – all of which had a profound impact on the political and cultural landscape. At the end of the century the American Revolution, French Revolution and Industrial Revolution, perhaps three of the most significant events in modern history, set in motion developments that eventually dominated world political, economic, and social life.

In a groundbreaking effort, Gale initiated a revolution of its own: digitization of epic proportions to preserve these invaluable works in the largest online archive of its kind. Contributions from major world libraries constitute over 175,000 original printed works. Scanned images of the actual pages, rather than transcriptions, recreate the works *as they first appeared.*

Now for the first time, these high-quality digital scans of original works are available via print-on-demand, making them readily accessible to libraries, students, independent scholars, and readers of all ages.

For our initial release we have created seven robust collections to form one the world's most comprehensive catalogs of 18th century works.

Initial Gale ECCO Print Editions collections include:

History and Geography
Rich in titles on English life and social history, this collection spans the world as it was known to eighteenth-century historians and explorers. Titles include a wealth of travel accounts and diaries, histories of nations from throughout the world, and maps and charts of a world that was still being discovered. Students of the War of American Independence will find fascinating accounts from the British side of conflict.

Social Science

Delve into what it was like to live during the eighteenth century by reading the first-hand accounts of everyday people, including city dwellers and farmers, businessmen and bankers, artisans and merchants, artists and their patrons, politicians and their constituents. Original texts make the American, French, and Industrial revolutions vividly contemporary.

Medicine, Science and Technology

Medical theory and practice of the 1700s developed rapidly, as is evidenced by the extensive collection, which includes descriptions of diseases, their conditions, and treatments. Books on science and technology, agriculture, military technology, natural philosophy, even cookbooks, are all contained here.

Literature and Language

Western literary study flows out of eighteenth-century works by Alexander Pope, Daniel Defoe, Henry Fielding, Frances Burney, Denis Diderot, Johann Gottfried Herder, Johann Wolfgang von Goethe, and others. Experience the birth of the modern novel, or compare the development of language using dictionaries and grammar discourses.

Religion and Philosophy

The Age of Enlightenment profoundly enriched religious and philosophical understanding and continues to influence present-day thinking. Works collected here include masterpieces by David Hume, Immanuel Kant, and Jean-Jacques Rousseau, as well as religious sermons and moral debates on the issues of the day, such as the slave trade. The Age of Reason saw conflict between Protestantism and Catholicism transformed into one between faith and logic -- a debate that continues in the twenty-first century.

Law and Reference

This collection reveals the history of English common law and Empire law in a vastly changing world of British expansion. Dominating the legal field is the *Commentaries of the Law of England* by Sir William Blackstone, which first appeared in 1765. Reference works such as almanacs and catalogues continue to educate us by revealing the day-to-day workings of society.

Fine Arts

The eighteenth-century fascination with Greek and Roman antiquity followed the systematic excavation of the ruins at Pompeii and Herculaneum in southern Italy; and after 1750 a neoclassical style dominated all artistic fields. The titles here trace developments in mostly English-language works on painting, sculpture, architecture, music, theater, and other disciplines. Instructional works on musical instruments, catalogs of art objects, comic operas, and more are also included.

The BiblioLife Network

This project was made possible in part by the BiblioLife Network (BLN), a project aimed at addressing some of the huge challenges facing book preservationists around the world. The BLN includes libraries, library networks, archives, subject matter experts, online communities and library service providers. We believe every book ever published should be available as a high-quality print reproduction; printed on-demand anywhere in the world. This insures the ongoing accessibility of the content and helps generate sustainable revenue for the libraries and organizations that work to preserve these important materials.

The following book is in the "public domain" and represents an authentic reproduction of the text as printed by the original publisher. While we have attempted to accurately maintain the integrity of the original work, there are sometimes problems with the original work or the micro-film from which the books were digitized. This can result in minor errors in reproduction. Possible imperfections include missing and blurred pages, poor pictures, markings and other reproduction issues beyond our control. Because this work is culturally important, we have made it available as part of our commitment to protecting, preserving, and promoting the world's literature.

GUIDE TO FOLD-OUTS MAPS and OVERSIZED IMAGES

The book you are reading was digitized from microfilm captured over the past thirty to forty years. Years after the creation of the original microfilm, the book was converted to digital files and made available in an online database.

In an online database, page images do not need to conform to the size restrictions found in a printed book. When converting these images back into a printed bound book, the page sizes are standardized in ways that maintain the detail of the original. For large images, such as fold-out maps, the original page image is split into two or more pages

Guidelines used to determine how to split the page image follows:

• Some images are split vertically; large images require vertical and horizontal splits.
• For horizontal splits, the content is split left to right.
• For vertical splits, the content is split from top to bottom.
• For both vertical and horizontal splits, the image is processed from top left to bottom right.

HIS GRACE

THE

Duke of Wharton's

SPEECH

IN THE

HOUSE *of* LORDS,

ON THE

Third Reading of the BILL *to*
Inflict Pains and Penalties on FRANCIS
(late) Lord Bishop of ROCHESTER;

MAY *the* 15*th*, 1723.

LONDON:

Printed for T. WARNER, at the *Black-Boy*, in *Pater-
Noster-Row.* 1723.   [Price 1 *s.* 6 *d.*]

THE

Duke of Wharton's

SPEECH

IN THE

HOUSE OF LORDS, &c.

OME Words which have fallen from the Reverend Pre-late, who fpoke laft, have made it, in fome meafure, neceffary for me to trouble your Lordfhips with the Rea-fons that induced me to differ with him in Opinion, and to give my Negative to the Bill now depending be-fore us.

If I don't mif-underftand his Lordfhip (and if I fhould miftake his Meaning, I hope he will fet me right) he was pleafed to fay, That Perfons without Doors would be apt to caft different Reflections on the particular Behaviour of every Lord this Day; That thofe who were for the paffing of this Bill, would be accufed of Malice and Partiality; And thofe who were of contrary Sentiments, would be branded with Difaffection to the prefent Happy Eftablifhment.

For my Part, I am far from thinking, that Confiderations of this Nature will have the leaft Weight with any of your Lordfhips; and am very certain, that every one, who gives his Vote on this important Occafion, has attended, with the greateft Care, to the Evidence that has been given at your Bar, which is the Foundation of this Day's Debate.

The Proofs that have been brought to fupport the Charge, and the Bifhop's Defence, are to be thoroughly confidered; and when your Lordfhips proceed ac-cording to the Rules of Juftice, you will not fear, nor value, any Confequences which may attend the difcharging of your Duty.

So far I will venture to affirm, That the best Way to shew our Zeal to His Majesty, and the present Government, is, To act, in all Cases, both in our Judicial and Legislative Capacities, with that Honour and Impartiality as ought to flourish in this great Council of the Nation.

I could have wished, the Noble Lords who have given their Reasons for the passing this extraordinary Law, would have entred into the particular Circumstances of this Case, and considered it singly on its own Merits; But instead of speaking on that Head, I cannot but take Notice, That they have wandered from that (which ought to have been their only Consideration) into Learned Discourses on Bills of this Nature in General.

I shall not trouble this House with any Arguments against Attainders. Many Lords, of greater Weight and Abilities than myself, have already spoke fully to this Point in the preceding Debates.

I shall only, so far agree with the Reverend Prelate, who spoke before me, That it is proper, that such a Power of punishing by Bill, should be vested in the Legislature to be exercised on extraordinary Emergencies. But then I must add, If ever that Power is abused; if ever it is employed to destroy innocent Persons, it is evident, That the Lives, Liberties, and Fortunes of every Subject in *Britain*, are in the utmost Danger, and liable to be sacrificed to the Fury of a Party.

It has been admitted, That every Bill of Pains and Penalties is to stand upon its own Bottom; and that the passing of One Act of this Nature, is not to be brought as a Precedent for the supporting of Another, unless there be convincing Evidence to inforce each Case. And therefore the proper Consideration now before us, is, Whether the Evidence offer'd against the Unfortunate Prelate is sufficient to induce your Lordships to believe him Guilty of the heavy Crimes of which he stands accused?

My Lords, I shall take the Liberty of considering the whole Proofs that have been brought on this Occasion, both by Way of Charge, Defence, Reply, and Rejoynder; and though I own myself very unequal to this Task, yet, since no other Lord, who could do it much better, has undertaken it, I think it my Duty, as a Peer, and as an *Englishman*, to lay it before your Lordships in the best Manner I am able.

The Method I shall observe for the more clear Stating of the Case, shall be to lay every particular Branch of Evidence before you, and to distinguish the several Parts of the Accusation, and consider them separately, to avoid Confusion, and to be the more exact in what I have to offer.

I hope I shall have your Lordships Indulgence for taking up so much of your Time as this will require; But I assure you, I shall endeavour to be as brief as the Nature of the Thing will admit, and will intrude on your Patience as little as possible.

I must also desire your Lordships will pardon me, if I repeat several Arguments that have been used by the Council at the Bar; and if I even mention some Things which fell from me in the Debate on Mr. *Kelly's* Bill, whose Case is very much interwoven with the present; so that it is almost impossible to avoid it.

Before I go any further, I cannot but say, That were these Crimes plainly proved against the Bishop of *Rochester*, his sacred Function and Station in the Church, would be Aggravations of his Guilt: But, as this is certain on the one Hand; so on the other, your Lordships will require very clear Demonstration, before you can think it possible for a Bishop of the Protestant Church (who has signalized himself in Defence of the Reformation; and the only one of that Bench where he had lately the Honour of sitting, that ever wrote in Favour of *Martin Luther*) to engage into a Conspiracy for introducing Popery and Arbitrary Power amongst us.

My Lords, The Council for the Bill opened the Charge with acquainting the House, That it was only to be supported by producing of decyphered Letters full of Fictitious Names and Cant Words; They were so very fair as to confess, they had not one living Witness that could charge the Bishop with any thing, nor even so much as a Letter under his own Hand; Therefore, on the first View, this Manner of condemning, on such kind of Evidence, ought to require our utmost Caution, lest we should establish a Method, which our Enemies may hereafter take to destroy the Greatest and most Innocent Subject in the Kingdom.

Mr *Wearg* cited Two Cases, which he would willingly have us receive as Precedents to justify the admitting of Circumstantial Evidence: The one was, The Case of *Ashton*, who was condemned on Circumstances only; But, my Lords, This was before the Treason-Act was passed, which requires Two positive Witnesses, and nothing could induce the Legislature to pass that Law, but a thorough Conviction of the Danger that might attend the admitting of any Proofs which were not positive or certain.

The Second Case he cited, was that of *Harrison*, for the Murther of Dr. *Clinch*, and the Learned Gentleman tells you, that it was the pulling out of a Handkerchief that led to the Discovery of that Murder. It is very certain, Circumstances may lead to the Discovery of Evidence; But must be well supported before they can be converted into convincing Proofs.

The First Piece of Evidence that was offered at the Bar, was the Extracts of Letters from Abroad, which this House seems, in some measure, to have declared to be immaterial, when they did not so much as desire to see Copies of the whole Letters, nor the Originals, and even admitted one to be read which was Anonymous. But it will not be improper to observe, that through this whole Correspondence, the Bishop of *Rochester* is not named. And therefore I cannot see why they took up our Time with reading Papers quite Foreign from this Case; especially since every Body allows there has been a Conspiracy, which is the only Fact to be gathered from this Correspondence.

The next Point which was attempted to be proved, was, That Captain *Halstead* went to fetch the late Duke of *Ormond*, and was at the Deanary with the Bishop before he imbark'd; There are also Two Letters found in the Bishop's Close-stool from this Gentleman to his Lordship, which were read, and are only Appointments for Visits, but mention nothing of this Design, and, I think, there was a Coachman, that proved *Halstead* was an Hour with him some Days before he left *London*.

This, my Lords, was opened as a Matter of great Importance; But your Lordships must remember, that the supposed Design of *Halstead*'s bringing the late Duke of *Ormond* into *England*, is only proved by Hearsay. One of the Crew belonging to the Ship in which he went, has deposed, That it was the Common Report at *Bilboa*, that *Halstead* came there on that Errand.

How far common Fame is to prevail, I submit But if this Hearsay were true, is every Person who was an Hour with this Gentleman before his Departure, supposed to be privy to this Project? And what a strain'd Construction is it to insinuate, The Bishop of *Rochester* knew of his Intention, because he received a Visit from *Halstead*, who was a Tenant under his Bishoprick? And this is the

more

more extraordinary, since it has not been so much as pretended, that any Correspondence has passed between the Reverend Prelate and the late Duke.

They then produced Letters directed to one *Dunvil*, which were decyphered:
And Mr. *Wills* was examined to prove, that they were rightly and justly ex-
plained.

My Lords, It very well deserves your Lordships Consideration, how far this
kind of Evidence is to be admitted: It has appeared to your Lordships by the
Oath of Mr. *Wills* himself, that it is an Art which depends upon Conjecture; for
this Gentleman has confessed, that every Man is liable to a Mistake in this, as well
as in other Sciences. He tells you, that he and his Brother Decypherer varied in
One or Two Instances. He allows, that the *Chasms*, which they were forc'd to
leave in those Letters, might alter the Sense of them. And, therefore, I cannot
but think, that an Accusation grounded on such Proofs, is uncertain and precarious.

The Person who is the Decypherer, is not to be confuted, and what he says
must be taken for granted, because the Key cannot be produced with Safety to
the Publick; and, consequently (if his Conjectures be admitted to be Evidence)
our Lives and Fortunes must depend on the Skill and Honesty of Decypherers,
who may with Safety impose on the Legislature when there are not Means of con-
tradicting them for want of seeing their Key.

My LORDS, In the Case of *Coleman*, the Key was Printed, as has been
well-observed by the Council at the Bar, and I am very much surprized, That
Gentlemen of such Abilities and Integrity, as the Members of the Secret Com-
mittee in another Place (who were so exact as to print the *French* Originals to
the translated Letters, that the World might see how just and candid the
Prosecutors of the Plot were) did not, for the Satisfaction of the Publick, permit
us to see the Key in Print, on the Truth of which depends such a Chain of Con-
sequences.

I own myself intirely ignorant of this Art; But, as I should be very far
from condemning a Man on my own Conjecture, I should much less do it on
the Conjectures of others.

The Greatest Certainty Human Reason knows, is, A Mathematical Demonstration, and were I brought to your Lordships Bar to be try'd upon a Propo-
sition of Sir *Isaac Newton's*, which he upon Oath should swear to be true; I
would appeal to your Lordships, Whether I should not be unjustly condemned,
unless he produced his Demonstration, that I might have the Liberty of Enqui-
ring into the Truth of it, from Men of equal Skill?

I cannot think any Man will allow Evidence of this Nature to be good; But
if in this Case relating to the decyphered Letters to *Dunvil*, your Lordships
should admit it, there is nothing mentioned in them that can affect the Bishop,
neither is he at all nam'd in them, but they are only brought to prove the Conspiracy in *general*.

The Examinations of Mr. *Neyno* are the next Points that are laid before your
Lordships; And, indeed, I must do the Gentlemen at the Bar the Justice of
saying, That they forbore mentioning any thing of them, when they open'd the
Charge.

They were so sensible that such Proofs could not have the least Weight to
affect the Bishop, that though in the Case of Mr. *Kelly* they were produced
against him as very Material to support that Bill, yet they did not think proper to name them against the Bishop; which I am thoroughly persuaded, is
owing to what appeared at your Bar by the Examination of Mr. *Bingley*, and
the

the Universal Opinion which every Person seemed to have of the Villainy of Mr. Neyno's Transactions.

My LORDS, These Examinations were never signed by the Person, neither was he ever examin'd to 'em upon Oath. So that, were they of Consequence, and he a Person of Credit, they could not be admitted to affect any Person whatsoever, in any Court of Justice or Equity. I don't mean, That they could not be read according to the strict Rules of Westminster-Hall; which is admitted on all Sides they could not; But I dare affirm, That no Credit can be given to 'em on any Account whatsoever.

The Person was closely confin'd, and consequently in the Hands of the Government, so that he was at that Time under the greatest Apprehensions, which might, in some Measure, prevent him from speaking Truth, with that Sincerity and Candour, of which every Person ought to be Master, when he is examin'd on Matters of such nice Nature.

Though these Papers were intirely given up by the Council for the Bill, yet the Extract of them was read, and they are the visible Foundation of this Charge; and if they are insignificant, the whole Accusation falls to the Ground. For the whole Proof of the Bishop's Dictating to Mr. Kelly, depends on Mr. Neyno's bare Affirmation.

The whole of what Neyno says, or is supposed to say, is, That Mr. Kelly told him he wrote the Bishop's Letters for him; Mr. Kelly denies it, and Mr. Neyno was so Conscious that he had been guilty of many Crimes, that he endeavour'd to withdraw from Justice, and the Providence of God, it is said, intercepted him.

My LORDS, If you will consider the Improbabilities of this Evidence, although it were upon Oath, and signed by him, it cannot be supported. He tells you, That he was intrusted to draw up Memorials to the Regent, yet none of those have been produced, and yet it is apparent the Copies of them might, with Ease, have been obtained, if he had been as thoroughly pressed to deliver them, as he was to declare he wrote them.

These Memorials, he says, were wrote by the Order of Mr. Henry Watson, whom he takes to be the late Earl Marshall. And I am certain your Lordships don't think that Fact Material, when you came to a Resolution, That the Bishop of Rochester should not be at Liberty to ask, if Enquiry was made of the said Neyno, or if he gave any Satisfaction to the Lords of Council, touching that important Fact of Watson's, whom he took to be Earl Marshal, lying with him several Nights.

It was very well observed by a Learned Gentleman at the Bar, That nobody can believe the late Earl Marshal would have reposed so great a Confidence in a Person, who was intirely a Stranger to him, and of such little Note, and the Jacobite Party must be in a low Condition, when they make Use of such a Creature to write Papers of that Importance.

There is so much Improbability in this and other Points, and so much Contradiction in several Parts of his Examinations, that they appear to me, and must to all reasonable Men, as the Dictates of Fear, and not agreeable to Truth.

He mentions, That the Reverend Prelate, (for such I still may call him) had some Favours offer'd him by the Court; But that cannot be true, and must be added to the rest of these Absurdities.

But

But, My LORDS, what in my Opinion clears up all these Matters, and makes it impossible for me to give the least Credit to this, or any other Part of the Charge, are, The several Testimonies of *Bingley*, *Skeen*, and *Stewart*.

I must observe to your Lordships, That the Two First Persons, *Bingley* and *Skeen*, are actually now in separate Custodies; and consequently, could have no Communication one with another. The Third is at Liberty; but his Testimony is so thoroughly supported by Mr. *Gordon* and Mr. *Kynaston*, that no Doubt can arise as to the Veracity of it.

These Gentlemen, who are in the Hands of the Government, are under Hopes and Fears, and therefore, it is certain, when they speak a Language, which, perhaps, may be disagreeable to those on whom they at present chiefly depend, it must be the Spirit of Truth that prevails.

Mr. *Bingley* was before us in the Case of *Kelly*, and was also examin'd at the Bar of the House of Commons, though not upon Oath; and though he has been more severely treated, as he told your Lordships, and more strictly confined since his first Examination, yet he has persisted in his Story; And though he was so long at your Bar, and so many Questions put to him, yet he never varied in any one Circumstance, but appeared consistent through the whole Course of his Behaviour.

I shall not detain your Lordships with Recapitulating his whole Evidence, for I did it very fully on a former Occasion. But your Lordships will remember, he told you, *Neyno* abounded in Money, which *Neyno* said (after he was apprehended at *Deal*) *An Honourable Person* (and on this Occasion, I hope, I may Name him) Mr. *Walpole*, gave him and more particularly, he mentions 50 *l.* which *Neyno* said he received the Night before he went to *France*.

Bingley told your Lordships, That Neyno *had assured him, he used to meet this Honourable Person in the Stable-Yard at* Chelsea; And, my LORDS, The Errand on which he was going to *France*, was, To discover some Secrets relating to Cyphers, which he would have ingaged *Bingley* to have done for him; and particularly, to get them, if possible, out of Mr. *Kelly*; *Which, he said, could he obtain, would be of great Advantage to him.*

That *Neyno* had declared to him, *He would be even with Mr.* Kelly, *before he was aware of it,* or Words to that Effect, and that Mr. *Kelly* always seem'd averse to any Acquaintance with Mr. *Neyno*, of whom he entertained a mean Opinion.

That *Neyno*'s Father refused him Money, which makes it highly probable that his Poverty was the Occasion of his Villainy; and that when he was taken at *Deal*, he had declared to him, *Mr.* Walpole *expected to find the Plot about him; and since Mr.* Walpole *could not, he must make one for him.*

Neyno told *Bingley*, *That this Honourable Person had vowed Destruction to the Bishop of* Rochester, *by saying, He would pull down the Pride of this Haughty Prelate;* which is sufficient to convince your Lordships how little Regard ought to be had to the Hearsay Evidence of so false a Wretch.

Mr. *Bingley* says, That Part of this Account he had given to the Lords of the Council: and I could have wished, that his Examination (as well as some others to the same Purpose, which were taken about the same Time) had been laid before the Parliament.

Mr. *Skeen*, who is also in Custody, has deposed, That he lay in the same House with *Neyno*, and had some Conversations with him.

That

That *Neyno* had told him, *What he had said of the Bishop of* Rochester *was intirely false.* And,

That Mr. Walpole *had offer'd him a considerable Annuity to turn Evidence; and had given him Instructions before he was called in to the Lords, what Questions would be asked him, and what Answers he should make; and threatned him with* Newgate *if he would not comply.*

Skeen says further, *That* Neyno *swore* (and I hope the Reverend Bench will, in such a Case, permit me to repeat the Words) *by God, there were two Plots; One of Mr.* Walpole*'s, against the Protesting Lords, and one of his, to bite Mr.* Walpole *of Money;* And this seems to be the only Time, that ever Mr. *Neyno* averr'd any Thing upon Oath.

To convince the World, what a Creature this *Neyno* was, he tells *Skeen* further, *That once at Lord* Townshend*'s Office, he had a great Inclination to have Stabb'd the Chancellor of the Exchequer.* He tells you, That *Neyno* had wrote a Paper to declare, *That all he had said of Lord* Orrory *was false.*

My LORDS, The next Witness was Mr. Stewart, who was unfortunately in Custody when *Neyno* was brought to Town from *Deal*.

Stewart says, That he slept the second Night with *Neyno*. That *Neyno* had told him *what he had said of the Bishop, was False; and that Mr.* Walpole *had offered him a great Sum of Money, if he would Swear to what he said, and turn Evidence, which he declared he could not do.*

That Mr. Walpole *had taken him into another Room before he was Examined, and told him what Questions he would probably be asked, and what Answers he should give.*

He says, That *Neyno* told him also, *That he had like to have kill'd Mr.* Walpole, *and so put an End to the Plot.* And that Mr. Walpole *had given him a Paper of Directions, which he was to Answer, in order to be a Witness against the Protesting Lords.*

As a Confirmation of his Testimony, Stewart says, He told this to Mr *Gordon* before Mr. *Neyno* was drowned, and to Mr. *Kynaston* before the Meeting of the Parliament.

Mr. *Gordon* confirms this Part of his Evidence, and assures your Lordships, That he had heard it from *Stewart* before the Death of *Neyno*. And Mr. *Kynaston*, a Gentleman of an undoubted Character, lately a Member of Parliament for *Shrewsbury*, has assured your Lordship, That he was acquainted with *Stewart*'s Account of *Neyno* before the Meeting of the Parliament; And adds this Circumstance, That when in the *Appendix* he saw those Six Questions printed, he shew'd 'em to *Stewart*, who seem'd rejoyced, and said, *You see, Sir, what I told you is true.*

Such concurring Testimonies from Persons kept so separate, and who are speaking against their own Private Interest, must have the greatest Weight, and must at least prevent any Rational and Impartial Person from giving the least Credit to the bare Hearsay of this *Philip Neyno*.

If any doubt could remain, as to the Validity of this Testimony, it is sufficiently confirm'd by the Persons brought to disprove it.

The Chancellor of the Exchequer himself, does not pretend to deny that *Neyno* told these Things, but only adds other Circumstances to Convince you of *Neyno*'s Villainy; and assures you, That at the Time he was receiving Favours from him, he was thoroughly convinc'd he intended to cheat him, which was the Occasion of his being apprehended.

He

He own'd the Transactions between them before *Neyno* went to *France*, and particularly the Money mention'd by *Bingley*, which are Proofs that *Neyno* must have disclosed these Secrets, since they could not come from Mr. *Walpole*, and He and *Neyno* only were privy to it.

Mr. *Walpole* has shewn your Lordships the foul Draught of the Questions mention'd by *Stewart*; and when he denies that Part of *Neyno*'s Declaration relating to the Instructions given him before the Examinations, He owns, he was twice alone with him; once the first Night of his being brought to Town, and the second time, when he gave him the Paper of Directions, which might be Foundation enough for *Neyno* to frame so Notorious a Falsehood.

The Witnesses brought by the Council for the Bill, to the Character of Mr. *Bingley*, seem rather to confirm it than otherwise; and all agree, they never heard any thing against his Morality. —— They indeed have said, he bore the Character of a *Jacobite*; and suffered for having dispersed a Libel. But Mr. Baron *Gilbert*, who was his Judge when that Punishment was inflicted on him, has told your Lordships, That his private Life was not vilified at his Trial, and that neither Perjury or Forgery was ever laid to his Door.

Though the Punishment he suffered was the Pillory, yet it is the Crime, and not the Punishment, that makes the Ignominy, and for this I can Appeal to the Learned Judges.

In order to destroy the Evidence of Mr. *Skeen*, they produced one *Pancier*, who tells you, That *Skeen* had revealed many Secrets to him relating to the Plot; and particularly of a Military Chest, which was collected to carry on these supposed Designs, and support the *Jacobites*. —— But I presume every Body who heard the Two Persons at the Bar, could not but remark the Steadiness with which Mr. *Skeen* denied these Asseverations, and the Confusion with which the other affirm'd them.

Mr. *Pancier* seem'd to drop something which intirely destroys any Credit that could be given to him, by saying, That he had owned to Mr. *Skeen*, That he was a Friend to this Administration; and yet has Sworn, That after such a Declaration, *Skeen* had still persisted in his Story, and revealed some Part of this Intelligence to him. How far this is probable, your Lordships are the best Judges.

Mr. *Pancier* goes further, and tells you, That Part of this Conversation happened in St. *James*'s Park, in the Presence of one *Dufour*. This *Dufour* was in the Hands of the Government, and I can't conceive why we have never seen him or his Depositions, when it would have been so easy to have brought this corroborating Witness to Mr. *Pancier*'s Testimony.

I can't but think, That the not producing this Man's Evidence, is a strong Circumstance to convince your Lordships he did not agree in the same Story with Mr. *Pancier*.

They also produced *Skeen*'s Attainder for the *Preston Rebellion*. But there have been many Acts of Grace since, so that he is capable of being an Evidence, and there has nothing appeared to traduce his Character as a Man of Morals.

In order to shew your Lordships, That *Neyno* could not possibly make these Confessions to Mr *Skeen* and Mr *Stewart*, the Council for the Bill, maintain, That they will prove *Neyno* and the Prisoners were not together after the first Night.

This, my Lords, would be very Material, but I think it appears, by the Proofs brought to support this Assertion, That they frequently have conversed one with another

The

The first Witness they call'd, was Mr. *Crawford* the Messenger, in whose House the Prisoners were in Custody; and, my Lords, I can't but say, it seems very odd, they should bring a Man to Swear he had done his Duty: He has told your Lordships, That Lord *Townshend* had given him Orders, That *Neyno* should be close confined; and if, after that, it should appear, That he had neglected such Directions, there is no question but that he instantly, and deservedly, would have been removed out of his Imployment.

This Messenger, in this Situation, tells you, That after the first Night, they never convers'd, to the best of his Knowledge. That Mr *Skeen* call'd *Neyno* a Rogue of an Informer, and spoke in very hard Terms of him; which I indeed think it appears the Fellow well deserv'd.

Crawford says, That Mr. *Neyno* had some Paper, two Sheets of which he found missing. He likewise swears, That Mr. *Stewart* lay upon the Stairs; and owns, he had at that Time two Servant-Maids.

Mrs. *Crawford*, his Mother, swears, That, to the best of her Knowledge, the Prisoners were never together: That she kept the Keys of the Rooms herself, but used to send up the Maid, *Hannah Wright*, with the Dinner. —— Your Lordships will observe, that both this Woman and her Son, swear To the best of their Knowledge only, and are far from positive Witnesses.

Hannah Wright, when she was first call'd, spoke in the same Language with them, though she afterwards recollected herself better.

When the Bishop came to Rejoyn, *Francis Wood*, *Thomas Wood*, and Mr. *Russel* severally say, That this *Hannah Wright* had declared to them, That she used to let the Prisoners converse together whenever she had an Opportunity, which was when Mr. *Crawford* and his Mother were out of the Way; and that she used to stand upon the Stairs, and give Notice when any Person came, that they might retire into their several Rooms. And the other Maid, whose Name is *Christian*, has deposed, That *Hannah* gave the Key of *Neyno's* Room to *Stewart*, and several Times desired *Stewart* to go up to him, and that they were together an Hour or more. And when *Hannah* was call'd a second Time, she own'd she was turn'd away for Suspicion of having help'd *Neyno* in his Escape; That she has left *Skeen's* Door open, who lay near *Neyno*; and that there was a large Hole in *Neyno's* Door through which they might converse.

She said, That *Neyno* gave her a Paper, which she was to convey for him, but that it was taken out of her Bosom, and burnt by one of the Prisoners.

When Mr. *Stewart* said, That he sat upon *Neyno's* Bed the Second Night, and lay in the Garret where there was a Partition, but a Communication between 'em, *Hannah* said, She could not be positive to that, but believes it true.

Mr. *Crawford*, when he was call'd to that Point, according to his usual Custom, denies it To the best of his Knowledge.

Your Lordships will now judge, whether the greatest Credit is to be given to the Belief of a Messenger and his Mother, who are swearing that they did their Duty, or, to the positive Oaths of *Skeen*, *Stewart*, *Gordon*, *Kynaston*, *Francis Wood*, *Thomas Wood*, *Russel* and *Christian*, confirm'd by the Confession of *Hannah Wright*, when she came to be Cross-Examined and Confronted.

This, my Lords, concludes what has appear'd at the Bar, relating to Mr. *Neyno* and his Transactions, and I am pretty certain, every impartial Body must agree with me, That so far from giving the least Credit to what he says, there have appear'd such Circumstances in the Transactions which are now come to Light, that

D

must

must make the greatest Caution necessary, before we believe any other Part of the Charge.

Your Lordships will take Notice, That Mr. *Crawford* confesses Mr. *Neyno* had the Use of Paper, and found Two Sheets missing; and *Hannah Wright* owns she had a Paper from him, which was burnt by one of the Prisoners. This, my Lords, un-undoubtedly was the Paper relating to Lord *Orrory*, mentioned by *Skeen* in his Evidence.

My LORDS, I am now coming to the great and only Foundation remaining to support this Bill: If *Neyno*'s Hearsay, is not to be believ'd, which is the Proof that was offered to shew, that Mr. *Kelly* was the Bishop's Secretary, and used to write for him, and particularly, That the Bishop directed Three Letters, which were wrote in *Kelly*'s Hand, and transmitted to *France* under Cover to Monsieur *Gordon le Fils*.

Every Body must agree, that unless the dictating of these Letters be clearly prov'd, the Bishop ought to be acquitted; and when, hereafter, this great Affair comes to be canvass'd by Posterity, it will stand or fall as this Fact shall be strongly made appear.

They first read *Plunket*'s Cypher, and Mr. *Vanradike* attests it to be his Hand-writing.

When this Piece of Evidence was offer'd, People were at a loss to know what they intended to make of it, and little thought, that they should be drove to make use of *Jackson*, standing for the *Pretender* in that Cypher, to shew that the Letter directed to *Jackson* (one of the Three before mention'd affirm'd to be dictated by the Bishop of *Rochester* to Mr *Kelly*) was to the *Pretender*; I shall take notice of this extraordinary Proceeding when I come to consider those Letters. I shall only say now, That were Mr. *Plunket*'s Correspondence to be regarded, the Plot is of a very deep Nature, for he has had the Impudence to insinuate the most ridiculous Aspersions against the Greatest Men amongst us.

Three of his Letters were Read out of Cypher, in Two of which Mr. *Johnson* is named; that is Mr. *Kelly*; but neither Mr. *Kelly*, or the Bishop of *Rochester* are allowed Places in his Cypher, and consequently were not in an Association with him. *Johnson* is only spoke of by *Plunket*, when he is mentioning Domestick News, and in no other manner than might be in every News-Letter that went by the General Post.

My LORDS, in order to shew that the Three Letters sent under Cover to Mr *Gordon le Fils*, were Mr. *Kelly*'s Hand-writing, which they very justly thought was necessary to be made appear before they proved that the Bishop was concerned in them, they produced a Letter of the 20th of *August*, which a Clerk of the Post Office swears was stopt at the General Post Office.

To convince us this Letter is Mr. *Kelly*'s writing, *Hutchins* the Messenger says, To the best of his Knowledge, it is Mr. *Kelly*'s Hand, and at the same time owns, he never saw him write till after his Commitment, and then he stood by him while he wrote Two Letters, one to Lord *Townshend*, the other to Mr. *Delafaye*; Those Letters were produced at the Bar, and therefore every Lord in the House is as good a Judge of the Similitude as the Messenger, who has lately been restored into Favour, on what Account I cannot tell.

If Mr. *Kelly*, during his Confinement, counterfeited and disguised his Hand, then the Messenger's Evidence can't be of any Weight; and if he wrote as usual, then every Person is equally capable of framing an Opinion of it who sees the Three Letters.

The

' The next Witnefs, is *Malone*, who fwears, he has feen him direct Letters, but can't tell how long fince he faw him write, nor how often.

' The Perfons who contradict this Evidence are fo pofitive, fo clear, and fo concurring in their Teftimony, that no Doubt can rife upon it.

Mr. *Bingley*, when he was fhewn this Letter, fwears it is not like his Hand-writing.

Mr. *Brown*, a Peruke-Maker, well vers'd and acquainted with his Writing, when he was fhewn the Letter of the 20th of *Auguft*, and the Date of it hid, by the Counfel for the Bill (fo that he could not know what Paper it was before him) fwears, it is not his Hand-writing: When the Letter to *Delafaye* was produced, he declared, That was his Hand-writing: When another Paper was fhewn, I (think, it was the Marriage Articles) he faid, That was more like his Hand-writing than that of the 20th of *Auguft*, but he did not believe it was wrote by him; and when they queftion'd him upon the Letter to Lord *Townfhend*, he fwore it was Mr. *Kelly*'s Hand-writing.

Mr. *Pickering*, who had Occafion to know Mr. *Kelly*'s Hand, having lent him fome Money, and received feveral Notes and Letters from him during that Tranfaction, does agree with Mr. *Brown* in every particular and moft minute Circumftance; which is a clear and evident Proof, that this Letter of the 20th of *Auguft* was not wrote by Mr. *Kelly*.

The Difference, which they tell your Lordfhips, they obferve between the Cut of the Letters in that of the 20th of *Auguft* and the others, is, That one is longer and ftraiter, the other wider and fhorter, which is obvious to any Body that will look on both, and is a Confirmation of their Veracity.

The Profecutors of the Plot might have prov'd this better, and not have been driven to the Teftimony of a Meffenger to fupport this great Foundation of their Charge. It is notorious what Search they have made for Evidence of all kinds; and as Mr. *Kelly* was Educated in a College, they might eafily have found credible Witneffes to that Point, if thofe Letters had been wrote by him.

In the Cafe of Similitude of Hands, when it has been the moft clearly and pofitively proved, as on the Tryal of Colonel *Sidney*, it has been efteemed to be Cruel, that a Man fhould be convicted on fuch kind of Evidence; and the Attainder of that unfortunate Gentleman was reverfed for that Reafon.

In *Sidney*'s Tryal, his Bankers fwore, They ufed to pay Bills drawn by him in the Hand writing they were fhewn, and no Perfons could contradict them; and yet the Sentence againft him was a great Blemifh to that Reign. The Great Lord Chief Juftice *Holt*, in the Cafe of *Crosby*, refus'd to admit it; and the Lord Chief Baron *Bury*, on *Francia*'s Tryal, follow'd that Example.

At prefent, give me leave to fay, There is no Evidence that it is Mr. *Kelly*'s Hand, and there is pofitive Proof that it is not.—— Therefore, we who live under fo Equitable, Juft, and Happy a Government, can never Convict a Man, in thefe Days of Liberty, on fuch infufficient Conjectures.

They next produced the Three Letters, which, they would infinuate, were wrote by *Kelly*, and dictated by the Bifhop, which were mention'd by me before, and which were fworn by the Clerks of the Poft-Office, to have been ftopt going to *France*.

The

The Bishop defired to Examine them relating to thefe Letters being detain'd, and would fain have known who took them out of the Mail ; this he thought was proper for him to demand, fince he feem'd to infinuate, That he queftion'd their ever having been in the Poft-Office. But your Lordfhips would not fuffer any Enquiry to be made on this Head, and Voted it inconfiftent with the Publick Safety, and unneceffary for the Defence of the Prifoner, to permit any further Queftions to be afk'd in relation to this Important Affair.

Thefe Honeft Gentlemen, the Clerks of the Poft-Office, have depofed further, That the Papers produced, are True Copies of the Originals detain'd by them; though at the fame Time, they confefs, they never examin'd them after they had Copied them.

They pofitively fwore further, That the Originals were of the fame Hand with the Letter of the 20th of *Auguft*, tho' they affirm this barely upon Memory, never having mark'd any Letter in order to know it again; and one of 'em declared upon Oath, That he did not believe there could be fuch an Imitation of *Kelly's* Hand as could deceive him, though the whole Houfe agrees, That Hands may be Counterfeited fo as to deceive the Men that wrote them.

They own they never compared two Original Letters between the 24th of *Auguft* and 26th of *April*, though they might have ftopt a Letter one Poft, without Prejudice to the Government, in order to be more certain in their Evidence.

Thus, my Lords, fhould this Bill pafs, this great Man muft fall by the Dependance this Houfe muft have on the Memory of thefe Clerks.

Mr. *Lewis*, who has long ferv'd in the Secretary's Office, tells us, That frequently Letters and Seals ufed to be Counterfeited; and, in a more particular manner, by one *Brocket*, who excelled fo much in this Art, that he has cheated many Perfons, and has fo far deceived 'em, that they have not known his Copy from their own Originals.

When thefe Letters, thus attefted, came to be Read, they are in Cypher, fo that it muft again depend on the Honefty of a Decypherer, before they can poffibly be made Treafonable.

Mr. *Willi* declares, They were truly Decyphered according to the beft of his Judgment and Skill; and more particularly, that the Number 1378, which is fubfcribed to the Third Letter directed to *Jackfon*, ftands for the Letter R. But when fome Lords afk'd him a Queftion, which perhaps had he anfwered, might have proved him to be under a Miftake; he refufes to give an Anfwer, either in the Affirmative or Negative, for fear of Revealing his Art. Your Lordfhips thought proper to prevent any further Crofs-Examination of this Gentleman, by a Refolution.

Mr. *Wills* fays, He fhew'd thefe Letters decyphered to my Lord *Townfhend* before he communicated them to Mr. *Corbire*, who is a Clerk in the Secretaries-Office, and then he fays, That Mr. *Corbire* and he agreed.

Before thefe Letters can yet prejudice the Bifhop, the Cant Names in them, muft be explain'd according to the Key, which the Profecutors of the Plot have made; And In Order to it, we muft believe, That *Jackfon* ftands for the Pretender, becaufe Mr. *Plunket* gave him that Title in his Cypher. Can there be a greater Abfurdity than to imagine a Perfon of the Bifhop of *Rochefter's* Capacity, fhould borrow a Name of that Confequence, from fo infignificant a Wretch as *Plunket*, who it does not appear ever faw him?

In-

Indeed, the Council for the Bill did not read these Letters against the Bishop, since they had no Proof of his Dictating of them, and they were only read on Account of the general Conspiracy.

I must observe, It was a great Artifice of these Learned Gentlemen, Whenever there was a Piece of Evidence to which the Bishop objected, they constantly pretended, they produc'd it to the Plot in General ; for they knew it could not be admitted against the Reverend Prelate ; But yet when they came to sum up, they applied them to this Particular Case ; which is not agreeable to that Candour that is necessary on such Occasions.

If your Lordships should be of Opinion, that *Kelly* wrote 'em ; that they were stopp'd at the Post-Office ; that they were duly copied ; that they were truly decyphered, and the Cant Names explain'd ; yet still this cannot affect the Bishop, unless it be fix'd upon him that he dictated them : Two of them were sign'd *Jones* and *Illington*, and to induce your Lordships to believe the Bishop was Guilty, as they affirm'd, they endeavour to prove those Names must denote him . And, in Order to it, they read some Letters, affirm'd in the same Manner (as before mention'd) by the Clerks of the Post-Office, to be his Hand Writing ; But first they read a Cypher taken upon Mr. *Dennis Kelly*, and sworn by the Messenger *Hutchins* to be wrote by *George Kelly*.

I can observe nothing upon this Cypher, but that the Bishop of *Rochester* is not mention'd in it, which seems very extraordinary, and is not a Proof of the Reverend Prelate's being ingaged in a Conspiracy.

The Letters they read of Mr. *Kelly*, are of no Moment, and are only calculated to fix the Names of *Jones* and *Illington* upon the Bishop.

They give an Account of his Lady's Death, the Bishop's own Illness, his going to and from *Bromley*, and in some of them, the Dog *Harlequin* is mentioned.

It seems repugnant to Reason, that in a Treasonable Correspondence of this Importance, a Gentleman should venture his Life to give an Account of the State of one Person's private Affair, and entertain his Friends Abroad with no other Business in such a Tract of Time.

In the Letters directed to Mr. *Andrews* at the *Dog and Duck*, which are proved to have been received by Mr. *Kelly*, *Jones* and *Illington* are not named, and those in which we find them, were such as pass'd through the Post-Office, and were attested like those under Cover to *Gordon le Pils*.

It is not likely, that in a Transaction of so secret a Nature, Mr. *Kelly* should take such Pains to give such a Description as might give the least Room for a Suspicion that the Bishop was concerned ; much less to have mentioned so many Particulars, as it may be suggested he has done, if there could be any Possibility of wresting the Meaning of *Jones* and *Illington*, and interpreting of them to mean the Bishop.

William Wood, the Bishop's Coachman, is brought to prove the particular Times of the Bishop's being in or out of Town, in order to shew, that they agree with the Times mentioned of *Jones* and *Illington* in the intercepted Correspondence ; and he refreshes his Memory by a Book of *Memorandums*, which might have been destroyed, if it had been apprehended by the Bishop's Friends, that such Evidence could affect him.

E   What

What they next attempt, was to shew, That the Dog brought over by Mr. *Kelly* from *France*, and which Mrs. *Barnes* swears, That he once told her was for the Bishop of *Rochester*, was a strong Circumstance, to fix the Name of *Illington* on the Bishop.

My LORDS, Mrs. *Barnes*, who is under the Custody of a Messenger, is the only Witness to this Point, and what she says, is only Hearsay from *Kelly*: She owns that *Kelly* never told her so but once, and that was when she thought to have kept it for herself: And, indeed, it might be barely an Excuse to prevent his parting with it, for he had promised to bring her such a Present before he went to *France*.

She owns, that to her Knowledge, the Bishop never saw the Dog, nor sent any Message about it, which seems to be very extraordinary, that if this Present was of such great Consequence, he should not have had Curiosity enough, at least, to see it: An Affidavit was read from *Bermingham*, a Surgeon in *Paris*, which says, That he gave this Dog to Mr. *Kelly*, for Mrs. *Barnes*.

Before I leave this Circumstance of the Dog, it is proper to observe another great Improbability, which is, in a Letter wrote a few Days after the Death of the Bishop's Lady, it is said, Mrs *Illington* was in great Tribulation for the Loss of poor *Harlequin*; and can it be supposed, That at a Time when the Bishop was in Affliction for the Death of his Wife, he should indecently discover so much Grief for such a Trifle?

I think this is sufficient to convince any Person whatsoever, That this Correspondence is of a very extraordinary Nature.

Mrs. *Barnes* has told your Lordships, That Mr. *Kelly* came from *France* the 11th of *April*.

My LORDS, I am now come to the only Piece of Evidence that seems particularly levelled at the Bishop: Which is, The Proof that has been given of the Dictating those Letters; and unless this be clearly and plainly made appear, I cannot conceive that any Thing can be laid to this Prelate's Charge.

Unless it is evident, that the Bishop did dictate as alledged, I cannot think any of your Lordships can vote him Guilty according to the Rules of Justice; for no Man is safe either in his Life, Liberty or Fortune, if he may be deprived of either, on Account of a Correspondence, in which it does not appear he was concerned. Though your Lordships should so far credit the precarious Evidence. at your Bar, as to believe that *Jones* and *Illington* stood for the Bishop of *Rochester*; yet, unless it is plain, that it was with his Privity, it is certainly impossible this Bill should pass; And if it should, it will hereafter be in the Power of any two Men, one at Home, and one Abroad, to ruin the most innocent Person, by entring, without his Knowledge, into a Correspondence of this Nature.

If the being named in Treasonable Letters, be a Crime, though it does not appear it was with the Privity of such Persons, I will submit to your Lordships, how far Men of the greatest Zeal to the present Establishment, are to be affected by Mr. *Plunket*'s Insinuations.

No Man ought to suffer for the Suggestions of another Person, unless it appears he has given great Foundation for them. And in this Case, would it not be most extraordinary and most unjust, to punish this Reverend Prelate, for a Crime which there is no Proof he ever committed? I mean, the Dictating of these Letters. And if, on the other Hand, the unfortunate Circumstances of his

Affairs

Affairs has furnished him with Means of shewing, beyond Contradiction, that he could not be concern'd in the Letters of the 20th of *April*; That for a considerable Time before, he could not see Mr. *Kelly*; and that there never was an Intimacy between 'em; Then, My LORDS, I hope, every Man who gives his Vote for the Rejecting this Bill, has the strongest Evidence of his Side to support his Opinion; and need not be afraid or ashamed to own it here, or any where else.

This Part of the Evidence being of great Consequence, I must beg your Lordships Attention, whilst I recapitulate the Heads of it as clearly and distinctly, as possibly I can.

The First Witness they call'd, was *Flower*, a Chairman, who swears, That he carried *Kelly* twice or thrice to the Deanary; but that the Bishop was never at Home, and consequently did not see him. His Partner swore, He had carried him, with *Flower*, one of those Times.

The next Person produced, was a Porter, one *Vanlear*, who deposed, That he went about *Christmas* was Twelve-Months, twice, with Messages from *Kelly* to the Bishop; The last of which Times, he carried some *Beaver* Stockens; That the Bishop sent for him up Stairs, gave his Service to Mr. *Johnson*, and thank'd him for his Present.

Mrs. *Kilburne*, at whose House Mr. *Kelly* lodged, says, That once a Servant came from the Bishop, to know how Mr. *Johnson* did, and was sorry he could not have his Company at Dinner.

William Wood the Bishop's Coachman, says, He once stopp'd in *Bury-Street*, but does not know for what; and that the Bishop sent a Servant somewhere, who presently returned. And,

Lloyd, who keeps the *Star and Garter* in *Palace-Yard* has told us, That *Neyno* once came to his House, and told him, He staid for an ingenious Gentleman, who was gone to the Bishop of *Rochester*'s House.

This, my LORDS, is all the Proof they offered of this Intimacy, from which they would infer, That the Bishop dictated these Letters, and is consequently Guilty of the Crimes laid to his Charge.

If your Lordships consider what was produced on the other Side, I am sure you must agree there is no Foundation for this Assertion.

Mrs. *Kilburne* denies, to the best of her Knowledge, that the Bishop ever came to her House, or that his Coach ever stopp'd there, or ever was sent for *Kelly*.

That *Kelly* did not go out of Town, from the Time he came from *France*, 'till he was taken up, the 19th of *May*, and never lay out of her House one Night.

This, my Lords, was confirmed by her Maid *Anne Ellis*.

Mrs. *Barnes* says, She never heard of any Message from the Bishop to *Kelly*, nor ever had any Conversation with him about the Bishop.

William Wood the Coachman, who liv'd with the Bishop Four Years, has declared, that the Bishop of Rochester never sent him with his Coach to Bury Street to fetch any Person from thence; That there was no Stranger at Bromley for a Fortnight before his Lady died, which was the 26th of April; That no-body could come in a Coach, or on Horse-back, but he must know it; That he never saw such a Person as Mr. Kelly, 'till he was shewed him at the Tower; and, That the Bishop went ill of the Gout to Bromley the 12th of April, and did not return to London, 'till the 7th of May.

Malone, Mrs. Barnes's Servant, says, That she never saw the Bishop, or any of his Servants, with Mr. Kelly.

Thomas Grant, who has been the Bishop's Servant 9 Years, has declared, That the Bishop went to Bromley the 12th of April very ill of the Gout, and that no Stranger could come to him, from the Time he went to Bromley, 'till after his Wife's Death; That one or other of the Servants always sat up with him; And that no Person could visit him, but they must know it; for they were either in the same Room, or the next Room to him; and that no Stranger, except Dr. Aldrige and the Apothecary, came near him. Grant says, That he was forc'd to go to Town to attend at the Westminster Election of Scholars on the 21st of April, but left Beauchamp there, who came down for that Purpose on the 18th.

Beauchamp and Steen, who were the Two Servants that attended with Grant, swear the same thing.

Susannah Harvey, Sarah Jones, Thomas Farnden, Elizabeth Higginson, and all the Servants agree, That they never heard of any Person by the Name of Kelly or Johnson's being with the Bishop. And,

Mrs. Inglish, who took the Names of the Bishop's Visiters for many Years, does not remember, that she ever heard of such a Person as Kelly or Johnson. And I doubt not, but that every Lord must allow, that it is not possible to have a more clear, a more strong, or legal Proof to a Negative, than this is.

I must observe to your Lordships, that most of these Servants have been in strict Custody, and severely used, particularly Farnden, and yet your Lordship's see how unanimous they are in their Evidence, and their Testimony is so positive, that I cannot conceive any Person can suggest there was the least Intimacy between this Reverend Prelate and Mr. Kelly; and much less, that he could be with him to write the Letters that are dated the 19th of April.

Mr. Reeves did, indeed, so far agree, as to be of Opinion, that they might have been wrote the 11th of April, which was the Day Kelly came from France: But, my Lords, Mrs. Barnes has deposed, He went to Bed the Minute he came Home, and lay there for a considerable Time, Besides, it is improbable, that Letters wrote the 11th, should not be sent 'till the 19th. But if any further Argument was necessary to confute this absurd Supposition, The Earl of Sunderland's Death is mentioned in the Letter to Chivers, and that Noble Lord died the 19th, at which Time it has been prov'd, Mr. Kelly was not with the Bishop.

The Bishop of St. Asaph did, at first, peremptorily contradict one Part of Mr Grant's Evidence, by saying, He had received a Letter from the Bishop of Rochester at the Time which Grant has sworn he was so ill of the Gout that he could not write.

His Lordship positively affirmed, That he received this Letter on Saturday the 21st of April in the Morning, and saw Grant in London between Twelve and Two: But when it was proved that Grant did not leave Bromley 'till the Evening of that Day, and that another Person officiated for him as Butler in the Deanary, by Reason

fon of his Abfence, then the Bifhop feem'd to think himfelf under a Miftake, and allow'd it might have been fome time before.

His Lordfhip own'd, He never received a Letter from the Bifhop of *Rochefter* before nor fince, and therefore was a Stranger to his Hand.

I could have wifhed this Reverend Prelate had recollected himfelf more fully, before he had given his Teftimony in a Matter of this great Importance to one of his Brethren.

There was another Witnefs examined, which was *Crofton* the Shoemaker, to prove, that *Talbot* (who was faid to have received the Three Letters directed to *Gordon le Fils*) was at that Time in *London*, when he was fuppofed to have been in *Bologn*. *Crofton* fwears he faw him in Town the 29th of *April*, and prov'd it by his Book.

There was another Perfon call'd, whofe Name was *Donner*, that depofed, *Gordon* own'd to him the receiving of this Pacquet; But an Affidavit was produced from *Gordon*, in which he denies it. *Donner's* Evidence is only Hearfay, the other is pofitive.

My Lords, The Council for the Bill, produced fome Papers which were taken in the Bifhop's Cuftody when he was apprehended, and endeavour to draw very ill-natur'd and forc'd Conftructions from them.

The Firft was a Letter from the Dutchefs of *Ormond*, in which fhe acquaints him, *That fhe had fomething to fend him, which fhe could not truft to a better Hand;* or Words to that Effect. And this they would pretend to infinuate, were fome treafonable Papers.

I appeal to all Mankind, Whether it is not very extraordinary to fuppofe, that the Bifhop fhould be prefumed to convey a Traytorous Correfpondence thro' that Channel. Every-body knows the Friendfhip which was between the Reverend Prelate and that Family; and it is not furprizing that this unfortunate Lady fhould think him a proper Perfon to confult, and intruft with her own Affairs. Therefore I can't think, that thefe general Expreffions can at all affect him.

The next they read, is a Paper found, or pretended to be found, at the Deanary, fubfcribed to *Dubois*, but without Date; In this the Perfon who writes it, fays, He received a Letter by Mr. *Johnfon*, to which he return'd an Anfwer in his Hand.

The Secret-Committee, at firft, apprehended, that this was received by the Bifhop, and thus it pafs'd, 'till upon feizing a Letter wrote in the *Tower* by his Lordfhip, they found a Similitude in the Seals, which immediately inlightned them, and then it was prefently faid to have been wrote by the Bifhop.

They then wanted to fix this to be the Bifhop's own Hand-writing, and they could find no other Way of doing it, but pretending there was a Similitude between the E's in this Letter, and thofe which the Bifhop generally ufed. I believe it is the firft Time that ever fuch an Argument was brought to prove that the whole Letter has been wrote by a Perfon; much lefs was it ever pretended to be offered to a Court of Juftice againft any Prifoner whatfoever, But, I believe, there is no Man acquainted with the Bifhop's Hand, but fees it is not wrote by him.

They would alfo affirm, that when in this Letter the Bifhop is fuppofed to fay, That he returned an Anfwer in Mr *Johnfon's Hand*, it muft be underftood to be his *Hand-writing*; which, I muft confefs, does not at all appear to be a neceffary Con-

F

Conclusion; for he might deliver his Answer into Mr. *Johnson's* Hand, which, I think, is more natural to suppose than the other.

Your Lordships must judge, how improbable it is, that the Bishop should keep such a Letter by him, which he wrote himself; or that, when such Care is taken as the Prosecutors of the Plot themselves say, for preventing any Person's discovering the Intimacy between Mr. *Kelly* and him, such a Secret should be trusted in Writing, and even without a Cypher.————The Two Seals which gave this Turn, are *Cicero's* Heads, which are very common, and are to be found every where. They are one broke, the other whole, which must make it very difficult to judge of them; and it is allow'd, That, at best, it is but precarious Evidence.

If Mr. *Neyno* speaks Truth, when he said, The Bishop had Notice of the Storm that threatned him, I am certain, that this Paper, if it could have been apprehended of Consequence, would have been destroyed, But, I believe, it was impossible for him, or any-body else, to think it should meet with such an Explanation.

The next Letter they produced, which they seem'd to think material, was that which was seiz'd on his Servant going to Mr. *Morice*: In this he says, That the Evidence of *Plunket*, and those People, could not affect him; but as he does not mention Mr. *Kelly*, they would have it presumed, that this is a Proof, that *Kelly* could have said something of him, But, I think, this must appear to be a very ill-natur'd Assertion.

Your Lordships will consider, he was then writing to his Son-in-Law; and therefore no great Accuracy was necessary.

In another Place, he says, That if they impeach'd him, he should remain in Prison for some time; and this they would decypher to be an Implication of his Guilt.————But, in my poor Opinion, it is the Reverse; He seems to say, That if the Commons should be induced to send up an Impeachment against him, he was so satisfied of his own Innocence, and your Lordships Justice, that he thought the Confinement 'till his Tryal, would be the only Misfortune that could attend him. The Example of the Earl of *Oxford* was recent in his Memory, and might justly create in him a Fear of undergoing a long Imprisonment.

It is objected, That he, in this Letter, makes no Protestations of his Innocence: But if you will consider he writes to Mr. *Morice*, I believe every body will agree, That such Declarations were not necessary.

Mr. *Layer's* Attainder was read; but it does not appear, that the Bishop had any Correspondence with him; therefore I can't conceive why we were troubled with it.

My

My LORDS, I have now gone thorough the whole Evidence that is brought to justify this extraordinary Proceeding, and must observe the Steps that have been taken to procure all the possible Means to work the Destruction of this Great Man.

You have seen his very Servants confined, who, it does not appear, were guilty of the least Glympse of Treason.

Lawson, a Baker of *Bromley*, who appeared at your Bar, has been employ'd to examine the Persons in the Bishop's Neighbourhood, in order to find the least Particular that could amount to the Shadow of a Proof, and went so far as to offer *Wood* the Coachman, the Wages that were due to him, if he would have gone the Lengths that were required.

Mr. *Bingley* told us in the Case of *Kelly* (and as it has not been disproved, it is to be taken for granted) that a Warrant was shewn by the Messenger, sign'd by a Secretary of State, to carry him to *Newgate*, which he was told was unavoidable, unless he would own the Letter of the 20th of *August* to be Mr. *Kelly*'s Hand-writing; But it appeared the next Day to be nothing but in order to terrify him.

Mr. *Kelly* himself, has told your Lordships, That Mr. *Delafaye* offer'd him his own Terms, if he would have turn'd Evidence: And this was done to destroy the Bishop of *Rochester*; or, To speak in the Language mentioned at your Bar, *To pull down the Pride of this Haughty Prelate.*

Your Lordships may remember, That Mr. *Wearg* objects to the Bishop's Servants, because Two of them had Employments, as appears by his Lordship's own Letter; But, my Lords, When they were examined, they acquainted the House, that it was upon reading of the *Report*, that they re-collected the Bishop's Circumstances before the Death of his Wife. And if every Man, who has a Place under the Bishop, is not to be esteemed a Free Agent when he is upon Oath, I hope it will be allowed on the other Hand, That those who have Employments under the Government, ought not to be admitted; then all the Witnesses, that have been brought to support the Bill, from the Decypherer to the Messenger, will be discredited, and the whole Prosecution must fall to the Ground.

My LORDS, It has been a Hardship as has attended the Bishop, that he has been forc'd to prove a Negative; and the Difficulty has been the stronger upon him, that your Lordships have not permitted Mr. *Kelly* to be examin'd, as was moved by a Learned Lord in my Eye, and if the Gentleman had sworn what he so solemnly affirmed at your Bar, relating to this Affair, I can't conceive we could have had the least Debate.

The

The Noble Lords, who appear the moſt Zealous in this Proſecution, were thoſe who oppos'd the Examination of Mr. *Kelly*, which, in my poor Opinion, is a ſtrong Argument, That if he had been brought before us, he would have perſiſted in his Declarations of the Biſhop's Innocence.

The Reverend Prelate, has deſired of any Lord in the Adminiſtration, and even the Honourable Perſon who appear'd at your Bar, to declare, Whether any one ſingle Perſon had charg'd him (on their own Knowledge) of being guilty of any treaſonable Practice. And it has appeared to the contrary ; Therefore this whole Charge is founded upon the ſlight Circumſtances and improbable *Inuendo*'s before mention'd.

Another Objection, which was raiſed, is, That Mr. *Kelly* made Reſiſtance, when he was ſeiz'd, 'till he had burnt ſome of his Papers; But, my Lords, I don't ſee any Reaſon to lay this to the Charge of the Biſhop.

Kelly is to anſwer for his own Actions, and is unfortunately like to ſuffer for 'em , A Perſon of his Age, might have many Letters in his Cuſtody, which he did not care ſhould be ſeen, and yet of a different Nature from a Traytorous Correſpondence.

After this Evidence is conſidered, I cannot think your Lordſhips will eſtabliſh ſuch a Precedent, which hereafter may be employ'd to ruin the Greateſt amongſt you ; and if ever hereafter Pains and Penalties are unjuſtly inflicted on any Perſon, Poſterity will derive the Original of ſuch Bills, from the Proceedings of this Parliament; and what Opinion will be framed of us, ſhould this be paſſed into a Law, I ſubmit to every impartial Perſon.

It muſt be left to your Lordſhips Conſideration, Which will be of moſt fatal Conſequence to the Publick, The leaving this Precedent (of Condemning on ſuch kind of Evidence) like a Sword which your Enemies may take up when they pleaſe, or the Baniſhing the Biſhop of *Rocheſter*, in the Evening of his Days, who alone could do, in his ſingle Perſon, no Prejudice to the Conſtitution : If he were inclin'd to overturn it, as his Enemies ſuggeſt, he is in a better Situation Abroad, than at Home, to execute that Deſign, and direct the Counſels of the Diſaffected. The Ruin of one Man, will not heal the Wound, that the Paſſing of this Bill ſeems to make in the Government of this Kingdom.

It has been ſaid in the Debate, That the Biſhop ought to have made Proteſtations of his Zeal for his Majeſty and his Family ; But, I think he took the moſt ready Way of Performing his Duty, when he ſhew'd himſelf Innocent of the Crimes laid to his Charge.

If

If he had made Use of any Expressions, which those Lords blame him for omitting, the same *good Nature* would have call'd it *Hypocrisy*; and those who are displeas'd with his *Silence*, would have accused him of *Insincerity*.

My LORDS, This Bill seems as irregular in the Punishments it inflicts, as it is in its Foundation, and carries with it an unnatural Degree of Hardship.

It is Felony for his Children to correspond with him : And in this Circumstance, it is different from the only Bill that carries with it the least Resemblance of this : I mean, That for the Banishment of the Earl of *Clarendon*.

The Earl had flown from the Prosecution, and retired beyond Sea. The Charges against him were, principally, *For advising a Standing Army*; and another Article exhibited was, *That he had advised and procured divers of his Majesty's Subjects to be imprison'd against Law, in remote Islands, Garrisons, and other Places, thereby to prevent them of the Benefit of the Law, and to produce Precedents for the Imprisoning any other of his Majesty's Subjects in like Manner.*

The 7th Article against him, was, *That he had, in a short Time, gain'd to himself a greater Estate than can be imagin'd to be gain'd lawfully in so short a Time ; And contrary to his Oath, he hath procured several Grants under the Great Seal from his Majesty, for himself, and his Relations, of several of his Majesty's Lands, Hereditaments and Leases, to the Disprofit of his Majesty.*

There need not have been any Witnesses of these Crimes, for they were apparent, and every body knew that he was *Prime Minister*; Yet Sir *Francis Goodier*, upon that Debate in the House of Commons, declared the Sentiments which I express'd at the Beginning, *That he was not against Proceeding, but unsatisfy'd to do it without Witness, it being like Swearing* in verba Magistri.

Another great Man, upon the same Question, and an Ancestor to a Noble Lord near me, said, *That if the Parliament set aside Law in this Case, we should be happy to see Law declaring the Power of Parliaments.*

The Punishment for Corresponding with the Earl, was High-Treason, and then Two positive Witnesses were necessary to convict, But, in this Case, one Corrupt, Terrified, and Perjured Person, may take away the Life of the most Innocent Man.

There is another great Misfortune which this Bill brings upon the Bishop, which is, That he is incapable of receiving his Majesty's Pardon : This, my Lords, is an Entrenchment upon the Prerogative And what must make it the more severe in this Case, is, That His

G   Majesty's

Majesty's Inclinations to Mercy (which are the distinguishing Characters of his Life) are stop'd by this Law, which the unfortunate Prelate might have Hopes of receiving, when he had merited it, by a Dutiful Behaviour to the Country that had sent him to wander Abroad in Exile, and by his future Conduct have confirm'd, if possible, the Evidence he has given of his Innocence.

My Lords, in the Case of the Earl of *Danby*, your Lordships have declared, That his Banishment should be no Precedent, nor draw into Example for the Time to come, and have so enter'd it in your Journals.

It has been proved, That this Reverend Prelate was at the time that he was suspected to be acting in Treason, engaged in Studies of the most high Nature, which is a Circumstance that ought to have some Weight.

If this Bill pass into a Law, such Evidence is establish'd, and such a Method of Proceeding introduc'd, as must effectually render all that is dear to us Precarious, and if ever, hereafter, we should see a Wicked Administration, supported by a Corrupt Majority in Parliament, this Step, taken in these Times of Liberty, will be a sufficient Precedent to give a Colour of Justice to the Actions of those who should be wanton in Tyranny.

The Reverend Prelate, who spoke before me, mentions some Cases relating to Bills of Attainder, which, in my poor Opinion, differ very much from our present Question.

The Attainder of Sir *John Fenwick*, was only to supply the want of a Witness, who had deposed against him upon Oath before the Grand Jury, and who was spirited away by the Prisoner's Friends: But at present, your Lordships are to supply the Defect of Evidence, by condemning on improbable Conjecture. There was a Noble Lord in this House the other Day, I don't see him now, who made the greatest Figure in Opposition to that Bill: I wish we could have his Assistance on this Occasion.

My Lords, since that Reverend Prelate has quoted some Cases, he will permit me to remind him what has been formerly said upon Acts of Attainder, That such Bills, like *Sisyphus*'s Stone, have frequently roll'd back upon those that were the chief Promoters of them.

This prudential Argument should restrain us from being too forward with them at this Time of Day.

The Act for the Attainder of the Earl of *March*, pass'd, because he had been instrumental in procuring the Attainder of another Lord, under Pretence of a Letter, which the Record says, was no Evidence.

The

The Lord *Cromwell* is another known Inftance of this Obfervation . He was the firft who advifed this violent Proceeding in *Henry* the 8th's Time; and it is Remarkable, that the Advice he gave to the Ruin of Others, prov'd, not long after, fatal to himfelf.

I have now given your Lordfhips the Reafons why I am againft the Bill. I fear I have tired your Patience, and fhall therefore conclude with the Words of the Great Man I before mention'd, I mean, Sir *Heneage Finch*, in the Cafe of the Earl of *Clarendon* —— " We have an " Accufation upon Hearfay, and if it is not made good, the blackeft " Scandal Hell can invent, lies at our Doors.

F I N I S.

CPSIA information can be obtained
at www.ICGtesting.com
Printed in the USA
BVHW012001020119

536770BV00026B/122/P